From the author

WHAT SHALL WE DO WITH OUR SILVER?

WHAT SHALL WE DO WITH OUR SILVER?

A CONSIDERATION OF THE SITUATION CAUSED BY THE SILVER LEGISLATION OF FEBRUARY 12, 1878.

BY
THOMAS H. TALBOT,
BOSTON, MASS.

BOSTON:
CUPPLES, UPHAM & COMPANY,
Old Corner Bookstore.
1886.

Press of Stanley & Usher,
171 Devonshire St.
Boston.

WHAT SHALL WE DO WITH OUR SILVER?

THE act of February 28, 1878, authorized a monthly coinage of silver dollars, not more than four millions, and required a like coinage of not less than two millions. These silver dollars were to be of the weight of four hundred and twelve and a half grains of standard silver. These dollars, with all others theretofore coined by the United States of equal weight and fineness, were to be a legal tender, at their nominal value, for all debts and dues, public and private, except where otherwise stipulated in the contract. Except for the period of five years immediately preceding this enactment of 1878, during which, under the act of 1873, silver had lost its quality as legal tender for all sums above five dollars, such dollars — of the same weight of pure metal — had been like legal tender without limit, always from the date of the first coinage act under the Constitution of the United States, namely, April 2, 1792.

This was a rating of the value of silver to that of gold at very nearly 1 to 16. But the actual market price in London of silver compared with that of gold was at that time as 1 to 17.7+, and has not since increased.

Under this legislation, in the more than seven years of its operation ending October 1, 1885, there had been coined $210,759,431. And there remained in the treasury of the United States the sum of $165,483,721, and in circulation $45,275,710.

This legislation tends to produce two entirely separate effects: one of present practical inconvenience in daily business, and the other of future injury to the credit of our currency. It raises, it may be said, two propositions — a minor and a major.

Let us consider, first, the minor proposition, that relating to inconvenience: —.

I. THE DOLLAR AN INCONVENIENT COIN: NOT SUITED FOR LARGE PAYMENTS, NOR NEEDED FOR SMALL.

The dollar is a coin not suited to large payments — it is of too small value for that purpose. And the dollar of our present coinage is absolutely disabled from service in all international payments — and these are among the largest payments — by the fact that its legal value within the

United States is greater than its commercial value in the market of the world, London; for any value imparted to it merely by the laws of the United States has no authority in London, or anywhere else beyond the limits of our country.

This fact is an important element in the consideration of our monetary laws: one which our later legislators may not have heeded diligently. Good service has been done in calling attention to it by Mr. Edward Atkinson in two papers: one an address at the Annual Convention of the American Bankers' Association, September 23, 1885, at Chicago, and the other published in Bradstreet's of December 5 last.

The dollar, then, can serve as money at its legal value only within the United States, and here it is desired only for small payments at best.

Nay, the dollar is not a desirable coin for even small payments among the people of the United States. This people have, from early days, been accustomed to the use of paper for even small payments, as small certainly as one dollar. They have for years, for generations, been wonted to the use of bills of less amount than five dollars, down to twos and ones, such as are now authorized and current. Such bills, from their lightness, are much more convenient than silver dollars. The weight of silver coin makes its inconvenience felt before it reaches the sum of five dollars; and five dollars in silver is already becoming a frequent offer that must be accepted. Then, the small traders do now, or in a little further substitution of silver for small bills soon will, find in their drawers sums much larger than that. These sums must be handled, placed in safety for the night, and brought out again for use the next morning.

In cities and larger towns the place of safekeeping for these daily receipts would be in the banks; and the daily carriage back and forth of these sums in silver would soon be found to be burdensome in contrast with the carriage of the same amount in paper money. The process would be felt as a cumbersome process, actually incommoding the transaction of business, and in the long run, and on a wide scope, sensibly increasing its expense. It would be felt all the more because modern business has so long been conducted in a different manner, dispensing with this laborious process. It has been dispensed with, because another method, much easier and swifter, has, in well-advanced communities, been so regulated as to be practically safe.

In another address than that already mentioned, presented to the same convention of the Bankers' Association, a member of the Commercial Club of Boston writes as follows: —

Specie is always unsafe, difficult and expensive to handle. Every parcel of a thousand silver dollars weighs nearly sixty pounds.

Here is a sample of the way in which actual payment in silver dollars works: —

A house in a city dealing in commercial paper sold to a correspondent in another city not fifty miles away a note for not far from twenty-five hundred dollars. The paying party, doubtless driven thereto by the plethora of such coin and the scarcity of paper money, found it most convenient to make payment in silver dollars. These, strongly boxed, were sent by express. When received, the dollars were taken out, counted, and sorted, that bad coin might be rejected; and then the good coin — about one hundred and forty pounds' weight — was carried to the sub-treasury, and exchanged for its equivalent in paper.

If, however, there had been no attempt on the part of the national government, in the interest of silver, to deprive the people of a paper currency which they value and desire to have for use, this business would have been done in a different manner — by a check on a bank in the city of the selling party, or possibly by bank-bills or treasury-notes, either of which would have been bankable; and it was something bankable which was sought and finally obtained in the actual case. But with how much unnecessary labor! Out of the small commission which brokers receive in such transactions how much net profit would be left, if all payments were to be made thus?

The whole amount of United States notes of denominations less than five dollars in circulation on June 30, 1884, was $61,540,066. If this whole amount is to be withdrawn it will make way for only the same amount of silver dollars, or less than one third of the present coinage. Yet how severely would such a change fall upon the convenience of business! How frequent and loud would be the complaints of the scarcity of small bills! Whether private persons receiving money merely to pay it out again could afford to pay a premium for paper money over silver coin, there is no doubt that the community as a whole might well and wisely pay such premium, if thus the substitution of cumbrous silver dollars for convenient paper dollars, whose payment is properly secured, could be prevented.

The operation of the act authorizing the coinage of these silver dollars itself serves to show the almost universal preference for paper money over coin when the paper is equally as good as the coin. That act authorized certificates payable in silver dollars to be issued on the deposit of such coin. These certificates have been issued. And while only, as before stated, about forty-five millions of silver dollars were found out of the treasury October 1, 1885, there were outstanding against the treasury silver certificates to the amount of $93,646,266. Of this large amount the national banks held only the small sum of $2,274,650, leaving over ninety of these millions for actual circulation.

Clearly, if people are going to use the silver dollar at all, they prefer to use it in the form of paper. They would rather handle its representative than itself. There is high official recognition of this popular preference. Says the Treasurer of the United States in the last report from that office: —

> The further issue of silver certificates should be discontinued, as being both expensive and useless. Issued to aid in the circulation of the standard silver dollar, these certificates have actually proved to be a hindrance to the carrying out of this purpose, and the circulation of this coin can not be increased to any greater extent than at present without the suppression of the issue of these certificates. (p. 24.)

This evil of practical inconvenience, which is all that is now under consideration, would not be removed nor diminished by an increase of the amount of silver in the dollars to be put in circulation. Such an increase would obviate an objection hereafter to be considered: an objection which is to be brought out under the major proposition of this paper, now deferred. On the other hand, an increase of the weight of silver in each dollar, which would bring its market value to par with its legal value, would only make the coin more clumsy and cumbersome, and less fitted for actual circulation than it now is.

The fact is, silver dollars to any considerable amount are not wanted for actual circulation. So large a coin does not maintain its circulation in Great Britain or in France. A member of the Commercial Club of Boston, in the address from which an extract has already been given, writes as follows: —

> When we compare our silver coins with those of European States of commercial importance, noting, for example, those of Great Britain, and that their largest piece, the crown, of five shillings, is so rarely met with that it is a curiosity, and that the half-crown, the two-shilling, and the one-shilling pieces are the coins chiefly in use without inconvenience; and that in France the five-franc piece, the coin most similar to our own dollar, though held in burdensome numbers by that government, — an inheritance of the past, — is not abundant in circulation, being in great part superseded by the favorite gold ten-franc piece, one is led to ask, bearing in mind the convenience of our one and two-dollar notes those other nations do not possess, for what and why are these clumsy, unsightly, and unpopular dollars coined?

If it be that there is a demand for coined dollars to so large an amount as twenty-five millions, it is certain that there is no demand for two hundred millions. Later will be suggested a method of ascertaining the extent of this demand.

There is, it may be remarked, legislation of the United States that seems to recognize the dollar as not an indispensable coin. In 1853 it was found that, gold cheapening in relation to silver by the abundance of the production of gold in California, silver, the then undervalued metal (undervalued in the coinage law), was disappearing from the country. A reduction in the weight of silver coin was resorted to, but only in coins of less value than a dollar, it not being deemed important to retain this largest silver coin in our circulation. It was the fractional coins that were most important to the public convenience.

From this reduction of the minor silver coins no evil seems to have arisen and no complaint. Indeed, it is to be noticed that it is not in connection with purely domestic payments, such as are, in general, all small payments — it is not in connection with these that the difference between the legal and the market value of our present silver dollars is, one day, to make itself most sensibly felt. This difference would not work a great evil provided, always provided, the number of these dollars was kept completely within the limits of the demand for domestic use. In this domestic use, that is, in small payments, money should have a certain, legal value, recognizable at sight. This certainty is a prime requisite: it is of more importance, within limits, than accuracy of actual value.

In foreign payments these conditions are reversed. Legal value, which is merely national and never international, there avails not. Our merchants do not need to be told that their payments to foreigners must be at par in the currency of the world. And the present par of silver in the currency of the world is its market price in London. This is the only value of that metal which will avail in foreign payments. Thus it is to be seen that, in two ways, our government has hindered silver from going abroad: it has put it into a form unsuited for large payments; also, it has given it a legal value which keeps it at home.

The former fact raises the minor proposition of this paper, relating to the matter of daily convenience, already developed. The latter involves the major proposition, that the coinage of silver dollars threatens, at no distant day, injury to the national currency, the consideration of which is now reached.

This major proposition is, that coinage under the act of February 28,

1878, tends to depreciate and discredit the paper currency of the United States. What the people of the United States want for actual, every-day use is, as has already been developed, a good paper currency. There is, and can be, no national administration strong enough long to resist this popular desire and demand. How the present coinage of silver dollars interferes with the convenient use of the smaller denominations of such a paper currency has already been considered. It is now to be shown that the same coinage tends to undermine the credit of the whole mass and body of that currency.

II. THE PRESENT COINAGE OF SILVER DOLLARS IS TAKING AWAY THE GOLD BASIS OF OUR NATIONAL PAPER CURRENCY.

Being lawful money, these silver dollars may serve in redemption of the United States legal-tender notes and also of our own national bank-notes; the latter, both directly and indirectly, as the bank-bills themselves, may be redeemed in legal-tender notes. Thus these dollars are, by law, made a part of the basis of our national paper currency.

The average market price, during the year ending June 30 last, of the standard silver (900 fine) contained in each of these silver dollars was between 84 and 85 cents; $84\frac{53408}{116363}$, or not quite $84\frac{1}{2}$ cents.

Our paper currency, it should be always remembered, has no intrinsic value. Its value is not material; it is moral. Its value is wholly representative, dependent upon how faithfully, and what, it represents. From January 1, 1879, it has represented gold, the legal value of such coin conforming to its price in the market of the world. It has been accepted as the representative of such coin, because the treasury of the United States has been ready to convert any sums, not less than fifty dollars, which were presented for that purpose into such coin. Prior to that date the treasury did not hold itself out as prepared to redeem this currency in gold coin, and, accordingly, gold stood at a premium. Gold, of course, will again stand at a premium when redemption in gold gives place to redemption in something less valuable than gold, nominal dollar for nominal dollar. And something less valuable is our present silver coinage.

To the substitution of this cheaper silver for the more precious gold, as the material with which to redeem our paper currency, the continued coinage of silver under the act of 1878, inevitably tends. The operation of this act is toward making the coin in the treasury more and more consist of silver dollars.

The great source of this tendency is first to be found in the frame of the act itself — in the feature which makes this Bland act of February, 1878, to differ from all other coinage acts of the United States. Other coinage acts had provided for the coinage of bullion brought to the mints, neither the bullion nor the coin made therefrom becoming the property of the government — still remaining the property of private persons. The first coinage act, that of 1792, provides that the Treasurer of the mint "shall receive from the Chief Coiner all the coins which shall have been struck, and shall pay or deliver them to the persons respectively to whom the same ought to be paid or delivered." The government did not assume the task of putting and keeping these coins in circulation. It left that to private persons, who found no difficulty in circulating the coin of our fathers, once it was stamped as lawful money of the United States.

But the Bland act has no such confidence in the coin which it calls into being. It does not feel safe in leaving either its coinage or it circulation to the action of private owners of bullion. It requires the government to purchase and become the owner of the bullion; and thus the government remains the owner of the dollars into which the bullion is coined. This is the mode of coinage which is provided by that act; and, apparently, it is the only mode in which any coinage has been executed thereunder. Apparently, the old privilege to private persons to bring to the mints bullion and to receive in lieu thereof coins of the same species of bullion which have been so delivered, weight for weight, of the pure metal therein contained, has not been allowed under that act. Nay, more, it has no existence under that act. The act contemplates the coinage only of such bullion as "the Secretary of the Treasury is authorized and directed to purchase from time to time." The Secretary of the Treasury must so purchase, and there must be coined at least two million dollars each and every month. To that extent the coinage contemplated by that statute is not free: it is compulsory. The Secretary is not left at liberty to coin or not to coin, according as there is, or is not, a demand for the coin named. He must purchase bullion and cause to be coined at least two million dollars per month.

And when this purchased bullion is turned into coin, the coins, of course, remain the coin of the United States. There is no private owner, as under earlier coinage acts, who will come and demand his own and take it away from the mint. It must remain in the care and custody of its public owner, the government of the United States. The statute, which caused its coinage, has secured no private interest to put it into circulation. It will move out of the treasury only as it is moved by the action of the government.

And such action has no power to keep it out of the treasury. Being made lawful money, it must, of course, be receivable for dues to the government; and thus an open way is provided for its return to the treasury. It does so return. Even when the mint has taken care to pay for silver bullion in silver coin, the silver coin thus put into circulation will not continue to circulate. In the last fiscal year there were withdrawn from circulation, United States notes of the denominations of one and two dollars, more than eleven millions, in order to make way for the circulation of these silver dollars with which the treasury was overflowing. And yet the President tells us in his message that these silver dollars would not stay out of the treasury: they made their way back into it through the open channels of the custom-houses.

The Treasurer, from his more special knowledge of the matter, states the same fact more fully. He says: —

> Every exertion has been made to give an extended circulation to these coins, but without the success which the large expenditure incurred would warrant. . . . Such measure of success as has obtained has been at a very great expense to the government, the excessive cost furnishing a strong argument against continuing the issue. The circulation obtained is short lived, the coins finding their way back immediately to the sub-treasuries, the return movement costing individual holders more for transportation than the original issue cost the government. As the sub-treasuries become overloaded with returned, and the mints with unissued, dollars, the government is obliged to transport them at a heavy cost to the nearest place in which vault-room can be found. (Report, 1885, p. 25.)

In a subsequent paragraph he states: —

> If the coinage of the silver dollars is to continue, a new vault will be needed in New York City, and additional vault-room in the treasury building at Washington. (*Ibid.* p. 26.)

The expense referred to by the Treasurer is an expense authorized by the act of March 3, 1885, making sundry civil appropriations: the expense of the transportation of silver coin from the treasury and sub-treasuries for the convenience of private owners — another anomalous feature in the present silver policy of the United States.

There is a fact to be contrasted with this, of the swift return to the treasury of silver dollars, as follows: After January 1, 1879, the greenback notes of the United States were, on presentation, convertible into gold coin, — the currency of the world, — and all so presented were so redeemed. And down to October 1, 1884, — more than five years, — only a little more than twelve millions were so presented and redeemed

— twelve out of three hundred and forty-six millions, or not four per cent. The rest were needed and kept in circulation; and later, these also.

This constant acquisition by the United States of silver coin which will not circulate, is beginning to show its effect on the treasure of the United States. In six years after the resumption of specie payments in 1879, gold was coined in the United States to the very large amount of three hundred and fifty-four millions. Yet, between September 30, 1879, and September 30, 1885, the treasure of gold owned by the United States fell off from $154,840,200 to $134,239,292.27, or more than twenty millions.

In the same period the treasure of silver so owned increased from $35,665,178.25 to $75,517,153.69, or near forty millions: more than doubling. Is not the present Treasurer fully justified when he reports that

> It is apparent that the execution of the coinage law is gradually converting the funds of the treasury into standard silver dollars?

It is true that the gold in the treasury now exceeds the reserve required by law to be held for the payment of the United States notes. And while those notes are kept at par with gold coin, they will undoubtedly be available in payment of the gold interest due from the government. One hundred millions of gold coin is undoubtedly ample for such a reserve in ordinary times when a feeling of public confidence prevails; but it may not be sufficient when such a feeling is exhausted. And confidence does begin to fail when there begins to arise an expectation, an impression, that gold is to be at a premium compared with other legal tender of the United States: a looking forward to such premium and a preparation therefor. And of this there is not wanting indication.

That the decrease of gold, along with the increase of silver, in the vaults of the treasury of the United States is due to some cause in that direction, operating solely upon that treasury, will appear if we see what has taken place during the same period in other vaults in our country not under the coercion of the silver act of 1878, as is the national treasury. The vaults of the national banks are referred to.

These banks are under no compulsion of law to buy silver bullion and turn it into coin. They are at liberty to consult their own selfish interest as to what material of lawful money they shall hold. And while the vaults of the United States have been losing gold, those of the national banks have been gaining the same precious metal.

Of gold in coin and United States gold certificates the national banks held October 2, 1879, $42,173,731.23, and on October 1, 1885, $157,-958,577.57, showing a meanwhile increase of $115,784,846.31. On the latter day the national banks owned more gold than did the treasury of the United States.

Yet these banks are not by law required to pay gold, against which payment they should store that metal. Their notes are redeemable in silver, and also in legal-tender notes. But they have deemed it wise and prudent to invest largely in gold; to lay up a vast store of that precious metal. It seems as though their directors anticipated a time in the near future when gold might be at a premium. If they do so anticipate, they can not be alone in that forecast. Other men of large business must share their anticipation.

To speak of gold as at a premium is to state the rest of the currency of the United States as below par: as at a discount. Now, a belief entertained by a large portion of the business community, that the national currency is losing its true level, or is surely approaching such loss, is itself an evil of great magnitude; one which has some power to produce what it anticipates. It is a depressing influence upon business. It is itself a want of confidence. There must be some apprehension of depreciation to our currency astir in the public mind; there must be some timidity abroad when a prominent senator, conversant with the currency policy of the government, finds it fit, on a public occasion, to advise against the purchase of gold within the next sixty days.[1]

But, aside from such anticipation, our national currency is surely sinking toward a lower level. The continued coinage of silver dollars which will not circulate, which steadily flow into the treasury, filling, as it is, the treasury vaults with that coin and emptying them of gold, must, at no distant time, reduce the government to the necessity of discharging its obligations in silver coin. This is equivalent to a suspension of payment in gold: a return of the national treasury to the status which it occupied prior to the resumption of specie payment in January, 1879.

If Congress is not willing to allow such suspension of payment; if that body means that the national credit and the national currency are to stand on the level to which they were brought by the resumption of specie payments eight years since, the coinage of silver dollars as caused by the act of 1878 must be brought to an end. The recommendation of the Secretary of the Treasury and of the President to that effect should be embodied in statute.

[1] As did Senator Alison at a recent banquet given by the Commercial Club of Boston.

This done, the question arises: What next? What shall be done with the silver dollars already coined? The whole mass may be considered as in the national treasury and owned by the United States. For, whatever may now be outside the treasury as coin or certificates must be redeemed by the government, in gold, at the value which the government has stamped upon this outstanding silver. So far the course is plain.

An offer to redeem in gold will result in the determination of the number of silver dollars which are actually needed for circulation, as the greenbacks are needed. That number will not be presented for redemption, as the great body of the greenbacks has not been presented.

Beyond this number there will ultimately be a very large amount in the treasury. These should not be issued in their present form, or with their present legal tender quality. They will practically have to be disposed of at their commercial value, of course, with due regard to the demands of the market. Whether means can be found to make such disposal less harmful than otherwise it would be to the interests involved will be considered in the following part of this paper.

III. THE COINAGE OF SILVER DOLLARS SHOULD CEASE, AND SILVER BARS AS NOW AUTHORIZED BY LAW SHOULD BE MADE LEGAL TENDER AT THEIR MARKET VALUE.

The main result which this article has reached thus far has been that the coinage of silver dollars under the act of February 26, 1878, ought at once to cease. That portion of the act which authorizes and compels such coinage ought to be repealed. This is the measure which is recommended by the President and by the Secretary of the Treasury to the consideration and adoption of Congress.

But it is, to use a common phrase, something easier said than done. It is easier to recommend it to Congress than to procure the enactment of the recommendation into United States statute. The Bland silver act was passed by a two-thirds majority of both houses of Congress over a presidential veto. There has been no indication that a majority in both those houses, in any subsequent Congress prior to the present, has been favorable to its repeal. The present Congress is reported as being not unlikeminded with its predecessors. Of course, behind these majorities of successive Congresses, there must be a strong support of public opinion, and undoubtedly there is.

Certainly there is in the United States a strong and very respectable public opinion in favor of recognizing silver as well as gold as material of lawful money. And in the United States it is not without something which looks like constitutional support. The Constitution does name materials of legal tender, and it names silver as such material. If it fixed, as was very generally believed, until decisions of the Supreme Court not yet twenty years old, that it fixed, what should be, exclusively, the material of legal tender, it did fix silver as one of two such materials. As this writer has said elsewhere, if the Constitution is metallic, it is certainly bi-metallic. In any view, however, of the constitutional provisions upon this subject, a very large proportion, probably a majority, of the people of the United States are bi-metallic in their opinions and wishes. And there is throughout the civilized world a strong public opinion, and it is not unenlightened, to the same purport — a public opinion entitled to great respect.

Under these circumstances it will be seen to be very difficult, probably impracticable, to procure any repeal of the silver legislation of 1878 which intends and operates an abandonment of the principle of bi-metallism, or restricts the legal-tender quality of silver to so small a sum as five dollars. If any of my readers differ with me here, if any of them believe that the present Congress can be brought to enact such repeal, they may not be interested in the following portions of this article. What more is here to be written will be addressed to those who recognize the difficulty above stated; to those who are willing to consult this strong feeling in favor of bi-metallism, in order to an avoidance of the evils attendant upon the continuance in force of the legislation of 1878.

The maintenance of that legislation is in nowise necessary to a well-regulated system of bi-metallism. It departs from the true principles of our coinage laws in two essential particulars; and it is in these particulars that the viciousness of its operation is to be found.

(1) It compels the treasury to buy and coin silver bullion.

There is no such provision of law in reference to gold; and before this act there never was any such provision in relation to silver, save as to subsidiary coin and the trade dollars of 1873. Our other coinage laws provide for coinage of bullion at the option of the private owners of bullion, those owners owning and taking away the coin into which the bullion is minted. Our coinage of silver ought to go back and be subject to that regulation.

The Secretary of the Treasury has laid stress, and none too much stress, upon this anomalous feature of the silver act of 1878.

This provision, which compels the Secretary of the Treasury to coin whether there is any demand for the coin or not, is the provision which has resulted in the overcoinage of unwanted coin.

(2) The act of 1878 is vicious in its rating of the value of silver.

In making this statement the important fact is not overlooked that this act requires the silver dollar, which it authorizes, to contain the same quantity of pure silver which was required by the earlier coinage acts; that is to say, those of 1837, 1834, and 1792. So far the dollar of 1878 is the dollar of our fathers.

And yet our fathers made their dollars upon a different principle from that upon which we are making ours. It is a case where a conformity in detail works a departure in principle. A case where tithe, mint, and cummin have undue reverence, and the weightier matters of the law are neglected.

The earlier statutes ascertained the value of silver at that rate, because that then was, or was supposed to be, its market value; the measure of value being looked for in the mutual ratio of the value of the two precious metals. And Congress altered the rating of coins into conformity with such market value whenever the difference between market and legal value was shown in the fact that the undervalued metal was disappearing from the country. None of those statutes attempted, in any substantive degree, to rate the precious metals other than according to their market value, except in relation to small coins where the difference works no practical injury.

The act of 1878 does fix a legal value of its own upon silver, differing from its market value in a substantive degree. The Director of the Mint, in his last report (October 9, 1885), states the average price for silver purchased during the year at \$0.98079 + per ounce standard; and the rate of issue of silver dollars at \$1.16$\frac{4}{11}$ per the same ounce, being an overvaluation by law of over eighteen cents per ounce — eighteen on ninety-eight cents. The net profits of this coinage aggregated, July 1, 1885, \$25,122,184.90. What justification can there be for a seignorage at such a rate, on so large a coinage as two hundred millions and constantly increasing?

It is undoubtedly the latter of these two provisions which gave rise to the former; that is to say, it was the extravagant seignorage which led to the confining of the privilege of coinage wholly to the government; and, so far as anything can be spoken of as correct in this legislation, the confining of this privilege may be so termed. Always when the seignorage was large the government has retained exclusively the privilege of coinage. Thus in 1792 the government was authorized to purchase the copper which was to be coined into cents and half-cents; and these coins were from the mint paid into the treasury of the United States, thence to issue into circulation. The same provision for the purchase of copper was reënacted in 1837.

With relation to silver, this provision is first found in the Act of 1853 and as touching only the coins of fractional parts of a dollar; which coins were by that Act reduced in weight from the rate of 412½ grains to that of 384 grains to the dollar. And with reference to these coins, the privilege of depositing bullion for coinage was expressly forbidden to all other persons than the Treasurer of the Mint. In 1873 the government retained the exclusive privilege of coining all coins — silver and copper — of less value than a dollar. This Act allowed private deposits of silver for coinage into trade dollars as for formation into bars; but these trade dollars were not made legal tender for any sum above five dollars, any more than the bars. In other words, the law affixed to them no value for any but trivial payments.

Thus it is plain that the uniform policy of the United States has been to retain to itself the privilege of coinage whenever the profit of coinage has been large; whenever the value by law affixed to the coins substantially exceeds the market value of the metal contained in the coins. And as before stated, this, considered by itself, is correct in practice; and it is clearly correct in principle not to open this privilege to all the world. Certainly it would not be good legislation for the United States to offer to all comers a legal value of $1.16 for every ounce of silver that they may bring to the mint of a market value of not more that ninety-eight cents.

The policy of the United States has been hitherto to allow free coinage only when the legal value of the coins has exceeded the market value of their contents, say merely by the expense of coinage, or when no legal value has been affixed to the product of the mint. And this policy ought not to be departed from. It is not in the line of former statutes to allow free coinage with an extravagant addition of legal value to the coin. Free coinage is, in principle and by precedent, inseparably connected with a close adherence to market value in the legal value of the coin. It is useless to attempt to walk in the footsteps of our fathers on one leg; and this is what an allowance of free coinage, with a legal value imparted to the coins widely exceeding the market value of the bullion contained therein, does attempt. If free coinage of silver is to be reëstablished, market value of silver coin must be reënacted.

It is now to be noticed that this substantive overvaluation of silver by our statute of 1878 has not enhanced its price. It has not even prevented its price from falling; from falling nearly twelve per cent. When that Act passed, the price (in London) of bar silver was about 55 pence per ounce, British standard (925 fine). The average price during the year ending June 30, 1885, for the same ounce, was 49.843 pence. Plainly, the Act of 1878, instead of raising, has not even stayed, the fall of the metal, to which it extended an unwonted and anomalous privilege.

Nor has this legislation, on our part, had any tendency to induce legislation favorable to silver on the part of European nations whose disuse of that metal had done much, as is generally supposed, toward depressing its price to its present low rate. There is no indication that it has influenced them toward the adoption of similar legislation. Indeed, it offers no basis for their agreement with the United States in the remonetization of silver, even if they should consent to consider that general question, or should come so far as to agree in general to such remonetization.

Those nations can not be expected to return to their former full use of silver as money, except in accordance with the principle which regulated their use of it as money, whenever it was so used by them. And that principle is the principle of a due regard to the market value of that metal.

If they would consent to remonetize silver at that rating, it ought to content our citizens who are interested in the price of silver. For they believe, and their belief is probably well founded, that a remonetization of that metal by European nations who have, to a large extent, demonetized it, would, of itself, by opening a new use for it, so increase the demand as speedily and permanently to enhance its price.

Hereupon this may be said. The friends of silver would be content to have the legal value of silver conform to its market value, as its market value will be, erelong, under certain contingencies. They are bound to accept such market value as soon as it shall have adjusted itself in freedom from those circumstances, supposed or hoped to be temporary, which now unfavorably affect it, namely, the unfriendly legislation of certain European nations; as soon as the favorable contingencies which they expect, namely, the abandonment of that unfriendly legislation, shall have been brought about. In fact, their best interest lies in bringing about this friendly action on the part of those European nations. And those nations would, according to their uniform previous action, if they made silver legal tender, be willing to rate it according to its market value for the time being—present or future. This, at least, might fairly be asked at their hands. Market value alone, then, furnishes any practicable basis of agreement upon this matter. The consensus of the civilized world can be obtained, at present, upon no other standard. Indeed, in the present condition of the silver market, it is impracticable to fix a ratio between gold and silver satisfactory to the interests involved. It seems unwise to attempt to establish such fixed, permanent ratio gauged and measured by statute. It should be left to establish itself.

Why not then adopt market value as such? *eo nomine?* That will be satisfactory to all other parties in this interest, now and in future; always in fine. And it will be satisfactory to those interested in silver in the near future as they assert.

True, market value is not a good basis for coinage: that is, certainly, for silver coinage; so small is the value of the largest silver coin. But it has already been shown that the coinage of silver has been carried to an amount far exceeding any demand for it in the present or any expected near future. Coinage can not afford a farther channel for the disposal of our future production of that metal to any considerable extent. For the requirements of small payments, the present supply is probably ample; and any increase required would, in any event, be of small value.

It is the matter of large payments which must be considered. If silver is to serve as material of payment to the widest extent possible, it must be fitted for use in large payments. The form best fitted for such use, as has already been stated, is not that of our largest silver coin, the dollar; largest not only actually, but also the largest which it is desirable there should be. The form of silver best fitted for such use is that of bars; their weight and fineness certified upon them by a government stamp, "with such devices impressed thereon [so the statute runs] as may be deemed expedient to prevent fraudulent imitation;" such bars, in chief, as the law has authorized to be made at the mints since February 21, 1853. To be made at the mint at the request of all bringers of silver bullion for that purpose. So read the original act, and so reads its reënactment. Here the coinage law has not departed from the old paths. Already, then, the law has provided the method by which silver may be thrown into a form suitable for a wider use than it now finds. Can the law offer any inducement to the owners of silver bullion to avail themselves to a larger extent, than they now do, of their lawful privilege without doing any detriment to the public welfare? If it can, it ought.

It can do so by making these bars to be legal tender. At least, the course of the friends of silver in reference to legislation by the United States indicates that such is their belief. And upon this point their opinion is to be consulted and accepted. What they desire is to be done, if it can be done without injury to the main body of our national currency.

Silver bars can be made legal tender without detriment to the Republic; without injury to the public credit or any undermining of the national currency. Our present silver dollars would work no such injury, if their legal value did not exceed their intrinsic value; if their rating as legal tender conformed to their actual price in the market of the world.

This might be done. It could not be done effectively by ascertaining what happens to be that market price on a given day, and enacting that as a permanent statute rating. For, from such a rating, the actual market price might at once begin to depart, either by falling or rising. The friends of silver expect a rise. Accordingly they object to such a permanent fixing by statute of the present depressed market price.

Their objection is well taken. The United States is not called to commit itself to holding the price of silver to its present low level or to any level low or high. Nor need it, in making silver bars to be legal tender. It may make the rating of silver as legal tender depend upon its market price for the time being; upon the day of payment; its market price *eo nomine*.

Let it be kept in mind that the consideration now is not of small payments, nor of the coin which serves to make small payments. It is of large payments, and of bars which may be used in large payments; payments above a statute minimum: payments which are, or are closely connected with, payments abroad. And in payments abroad, legal value (as has already been stated) does not avail.

This objection to the making of silver bars legal tender at their market value will undoubtedly be suggested. When this writer, early in 1884, advocated this plan in a communication which appeared in *The Boston Herald*, it was urged that market price was an element too uncertain, too varying from time to time, to support the important function of legal tender.

To this writer the fancy occurred that all who raised this objection might be quite young, that is to say, not old enough accurately to recall the state of things which existed prior to the resumption of specie payments by the United States treasury, January 1, 1879.

In the preceding years back to 1861 gold had had a market value different from its legal value, and fluctuating from day to day. But nobody, on that account, objected to the receipt of gold in payment of dues at its market value. Over and over again contracts were made to be paid in gold. How could this have been done if the whole business community were terrified from the handling of gold by its fluctuating market value? To the payee who wished to take no risk nothing was necessary save to inquire of his broker what was the price of gold, and to accept and afterward to turn over to him the precious metal at that price.

In fact, the market price of silver from day to day is not an obscure or doubtful element. It is ascertained by the Director of the Mint, as in London and New York, for every business day in the year.

That the same willingness to receive precious metal, in reliance upon its market value, still subsists as before 1879, appears from this fact: During the year ending June 30, 1884, gold bars to the value of $25,800,799.86 were sold by the Mint and Assay Office in exchange for gold coin, the bars being in demand for export. These bars had no legal value, even in this country; and if they had legal value here it would not avail whither they were exported. Here there was a sale by private owners of coin which had exact legal value, for bars which had only market value.

Again, during the following year, more gold was made into bars than into coin, all comers having their free choice as to the form in which their gold should be minted: the bars being to the amount of $32,027,463.02 against $24,861,123.50 of coin. And of silver, where the government monopolizes the privilege of coinage, private individuals found it for their interest to have manufactured bars amounting to $9,549,313.37.

Upon this point, of the practicability of silver bars serving as legal tender at their market value, perhaps the best opinion would be that of the men who have most to do with legal tender, that is, with enforcing the collection of debts, for it is there that the matter of legal tender comes in play. It is very doubtful whether this class would anticipate any difficulty in their vocation to arise from silver bars becoming legal tender at their market value. But, at worst, the evil would be merely an increase of litigation between private parties. And this would be an evil having no power to perpetuate itself. Any legislation producing that effect could be easily repealed; indeed, could not be kept long upon the statute book.

It is obvious that this measure could work no detriment to our representative currency. It would not cause it to represent anything which is not of intrinsic and adequate value. It would be legislation having in it no element which partakes of the fallacious theory of sanctioning what is known as "fiat money." On the other hand, it would establish only a hard money on a solid basis; as hard money as there is, on as solid basis as there can be — the basis of intrinsic value. Thus, it would serve to keep our representative currency on a par with the best currency of the world. What could better remove from the business community any distrust of the future which now tends to depress it? What could more inspire general confidence than a solemn declaration of United States statute that every United States dollar was, under all circumstances, to be made as good as, to be maintained on a par with, gold?

While thus working no depreciation of our paper currency, this measure would, however, restore silver to its place as material of unlimited legal tender. It would refuse to narrow the specie basis of our paper currency by excluding silver from service therein. It is certainly worthy of consideration, that so long as mankind have used the precious metals as money, they have used silver as one of them. From the dawn of history these two metals — both of them: silver equally with gold — have held this good preëminence. It is a very long experience, and ought not lightly to be departed from.

We may be told that there is no danger of a scarcity of gold: that its sum is, and will be, amply sufficient to serve the monetary wants of the world. But we are not called upon to take any risk in that matter. The assurances made to us may, or may not, be well founded. There is no strong reason compelling us to adopt and act upon them.

Such making of silver to be legal tender at its market value would be legislation which other nations might safely adopt. It would make no rating of value to which any of them could object. It would not, where that has been adopted, even interfere with the single — the gold standard. It would not ask such nations to recede from the position they have deliberately taken in favor of that gold standard. In the light of the latest intelligence which we have received of the views and intentions of the most important governments of Europe, through the official reports which the President has recently laid before Congress, it would seem to be, in principle, the only mode in which they would consent to return to the use of silver as material of unlimited legal tender, if they would so consent at all. They not thus consenting, it would place our monetary system under no disadvantage in connection with theirs. On the other hand, the perfect freedom in which our system would work under this measure would offer inducement to other nations to imitate our example in adopting it, which freedom would be in high contrast with the constraint and disability imposed upon the currency system of the United States by the silver act of 1878.

www.ingramcontent.com/pod-product-compliance
Lightning Source LLC
LaVergne TN
LVHW011146110826
845150LV00008B/2531
9781418192525